CURBSIDE SERVICE

Change the Way You and Your
Horse Think About Each Other

Book 2
From the *Toward Exceptional Horsemanship* series
Lauren Woodard

.

Neither the author, publishing company, nor any individual associated with this book accept responsibility for any applications or misapplications of the ideas or procedures presented herein. The author and publisher presumes in all instances that horse owners will solicit the services of a qualified trainer/ instructor if need be.

This book may not be reproduced in whole or in part, by any means (with the exception of short quotes for the purpose of review) without permission from the author.

lauren@**exceptionalhorsemanship.com**

Cover Photo is Courtney, the author's daughter, and her horse **Gryffindor.**

ISBN:1-4392-2214-2
ISBN-13:9781439222140

Dedication

To horses everywhere who wish their person understood them. And to horse owners and lovers who wish to better understand their horses and have an exceptional relationship with them.

Acknowledgements

Thanks to all the horses I've ever encountered for all your help and exploration.

Thanks also to my students and peers, mentors and instructors for helping me 'come to realize'.

Special thanks to Marcia Ketchum for all her editing help and clarifying. I literally couldn't have produced this book without her.

Thanks to all my friends who encouraged and helped, each in their own way.

That writer does the most, who gives his reader the most knowledge, and takes from him the least time

- Charles Colton

Table of Contents

1

What's It All About, Alfie?

You're on a ride in the mountains for the weekend with a bunch of friends. Everyone is saddled up and milling about trying to get on. Some are looking for a low spot and attempting to get the horse maneuvered into it. Others are trying to push their horse next to something to stand on and hoping he stays there. A few are doing the one legged hop while the horse dances in circles around them. Several swing up into the saddle while the horse walks or even trots off before they can haul him to a stop.

Meanwhile, you step up onto your trailer fender. Your horse walks quietly behind you on a long rein. As you climb up, your horse moves into position before you even turn around and stands perfectly square and stock-still with his saddle at your legs, ready for you to mount. You slide your leg over, adjust your clothing, maybe a touch to your hat, and look around at your friends as they watch with envy. A smile crosses your lips as you pick up your reins and waltz, I mean, walk off.

This is Curbside Service!

How many of you would like to have your horse give you this Curbside Service experience? How many of you would like to think about something and have your horse...do it? What would it take to get this Curbside Service for yourself? On one hand, not much at all. Could be five minutes to 2 hours. In the scheme of things, such as the time of your riding life, that's not much. On the other hand – for some, it could be a lot. The toughest part; it takes changing how you think! How you think about what you do. How you think about how you go about accomplishing it. How you think about your horse.

For many people changing what they think just isn't an option. "We've always done it this way." "This is how I was taught." The horsemanship/riding segment of the human population seems to be stuck in this thought process. Thankfully, the computer industry doesn't operate this way or we would still be using those first monstrous attempts at what would become our future laptops, iPods, etc. In what other business would the phrase "We've always done it this way" be acceptable?

Frequently, it's because no one ever introduced them to the possibilities. The joy and fascination of coming to realize the intelligence and capabilities of the horse are nothing short of marvelous. Changing how you perceive your horse and what you do when you're with him will inspire wonder in your riding experiences and the time you spend with your horse mounted, or not.

What if I could give you 35 hours or more of riding time per year?

Is it possible that you currently spend between 3-15 minutes positioning your dancing horse while you sort of try to get him to stand still while you mount? If you ride 3 times per week, that's thirty-one plus hours per year you'll *waste* while your horse is out of position, circling or walking or trotting off. Perhaps you've been riding 20 years and your horse doesn't stand perfectly still; you've wasted 620 hours. By investing as little as 15 minutes to 2 hours now, you can create a much more pleasurable and safe experience for both you and your horse. In addition, you will begin to acquire the skills and concepts for Exceptional Horsemanship.

The following procedure for Curbside Service and the concepts drawn from it give your horse a tremendous amount of respect for your savvy. This process will then yield fantastic results and benefit you in each and every endeavor with your horse.

Once you understand the concepts behind the skills, you can apply it to all your training. Your success rates will soar and time frames will change dramatically. Teaching is much more effective when you show, ask and allow. As with many tasks in life, it's usually easier to do it yourself than to teach someone how to do it. If you never teach the horse or person how to do the task, you are then required to do the task yourself each time you want it done. Instead, allow time for the teaching and learning and save yourself all that future "doing".

Boiled down, there are seven things a horse can do. He can move forward, backward, left, right, up, down or stand still. At certain times, the horse can do several of these movements in the span of a moment. Whether it's barrel racing, dressage, jumping, reining, pleasure show, trail, WHATEVER!!! It comes down to forward, backward, left, right, up, down OR, equally important, standing still!

Therefore, it would behoove each of us to make sure that we can move our horses' hooves in these six directions and ALSO no direction. Tougher yet, we need to do this one hoof/step alone, at a time, in each direction and with the selected hoof. You may think it's enough to get a horse's hoof to move, but is it the hoof you asked to move? Horses are plenty clever enough to move the other three before they move the one you're intending. And they are clever enough to move all three other hooves, but not the one you wanted to move. What if you're on a cliff? Or in a rusty pile of barbed wire? Might be just a tad more important there.

Consider that trotting around an arena is really one hoof here, one hoof there; all lined up and in a particular sequence and a particular time frame. It's easier to get the horse to trot around the arena than to move one particular hoof in a specific manner. Mainly, this is because we humans accept so much less precision in the trotting. Whereas, if you're asking one hoof to move somewhere...it either does or doesn't. Period.

How handy might this Curbside Service capability be if you need to, or want to open gates and such while mounted? Take your jacket off and toss it on the fence? Trim the mesquite tree while mounted so you know just how high to trim?

There is more on this concept in *It's Not the Task!,* another book in the *Toward Exceptional Horsemanship* series.

See just how savvy your horse is. He is fully capable of knowing exactly what to do and what is expected of him under different circumstances if he is given the chance to learn what you want. Open yourself up to the tremendous opportunities you have to accomplish more and better tasks with the help and partnership of your horse. The world of Exceptional Horsemanship awaits.

A man's mind, stretched by a new idea, never goes back to its original dimensions.

\- Oliver Wendell Holmes, Jr.

*As knowledge increases,
wonder deepens.*

- Charles Morgan

*The important thing about your
lot in life is whether you use it for
building or parking.*

2

What Do You Think?
How Do You Think?
Why Do You Think It?

*Thinking is the hardest work
there is, which is probably the
reason so few engage in it.*

- Henry Ford

Reality Check

Many people expect way too much of
their horse when they haven't given the
horse the tools and training to achieve
good results. Many times they haven't even
explained to the horse what they want

from him and still expect him to do it. For instance, if you want your horse to stand still, running him around at the trot or canter in a round pen to take the edge off, then saddling up and going for a ride isn't going to get the job done. If you want your horse to stand still, you have to take the time and teach him to...stand still! It is incredibly difficult for many people to stand still when they're with their horse. They feel they must be doing something to make their time worthwhile. But having a horse that stands still when you want him to is worthwhile. Don't just do something...stand there!

Some people never earn the horse's respect because they either don't care if the horse respects them or they assume the horse respects them. In many cases, this assumption is based on the fact that we have two legs. However, it isn't a valid assessment and it isn't safe or reasonable. The horse must be allowed an appropriate amount of time with clear instructions to learn what is expected in order to accomplish exceptional results.

At the same time, people also expect so little of their horse in other areas it boggles the mind. There are top Olympic jumpers and dressage horses, cow horses and reiners, not to mention "pleasure and show" horses that don't stand still for mounting. They can jump a five-foot course or perform Grand Prix dressage maneuvers yet can't stand still while being mounted.

This walking off happens because the riders are unaware of or don't care about, the ramifications of letting the horse do this and is the result of low expectations, training laziness and a lack of awareness. Awareness, consistency and precision are important here and should be taken care of as a basic training tenet. It's not something that should need to be addressed or ignored every time you work with your horse. If your horse didn't trot, would you address that? Of course! What's the difference?

Riders frequently aren't aware of the lack of training they allow and worse, foster, with their horses. The horses, however, are completely aware of what they can get away with. When some of these *trans-gressions* are pointed out, many riders scoff and deny the importance. You think! Why is it not important that the horse stand still while mounting, or walk behind his person?

Everyone has seen people leading a horse that keeps walking when the person stops. Meanwhile the person is tugging on the lead line. First off, the horse can't really be held or stopped with someone's hand on a rope, can it? A horse weighs in the area of 1100 pounds. Their average person weighs 160 pounds. Who is going to win this round?

Secondly, even though the horse fre-quently stops at some point, he's count-ing. One, two, three steps past, crowd my person and then I make them move their feet and bonus points if I step on one of their feet. Bingo! Does the horse know the person has stopped walking? Of course he does. Is the horse most likely cognizant of the fact that the person is tugging on the line and would like the horse to stop? Yes.

What Do You Think?

How many times have you seen some-one circle his or her horse around to get it back in place (for about 3 seconds)? The horse can't be in place without this cir-cling? Doesn't he stand still in his stall or out with his buddies in the pasture under a nice shady tree? Would a herd member run up ahead of the lead mare or stallion of the herd as they are running out in the wild? Never. If your horse is ahead of you...he's leading. Sometimes people let their horses nip them or their clothes and tear pockets looking for treats. Will you appreciate this when you're wearing your favorite outfit and his dirty nose is snuffling your clothes because he doesn't respect your space? Would you let another person invade your space like this?

*Make your next move from
where you actually are.*

- Frank Kuppner

These examples and others of their sort are not disobedience, however. The horse has never been told to do something in a certain way or not to do something. Therefore he can do as he pleases. He's a horse; he'll act like one. This is a lack of training. Unless you've made it clear that this isn't acceptable behavior, why should he decide it isn't?

Watching the 2008 equestrian Olympic events with the top riders from around THE WORLD not performing a halt at the end of the dressage routine is astounding. A required movement, or in this case non-movement, and yet these world-class horses don't do it. They don't halt, let alone stand and relax on a loose rein. Scoring reflects this transgression. The riders know this! The commentators always mentioned that the horse didn't actually halt. Canter pirouettes, one tempe changes across the diagonal and Piaffe. Check. Halt. Oops. Inexcusable.

What Do You Think?

*It doesn't matter how much
energy you put into something,
if you're working with the
wrong material.*

- Li Ao

Changing how you think takes courage and humility. It takes courage to even consider that how you've always done it may not be garnering the results you want. And the best way to assess how YOU are doing is to watch what the horse does when you do it. What is his response? What is his energy or agitation level? Is he thinking about what you're doing or reacting to what you're doing? Is there white around his eye or tension anywhere in his body? Just because a horse does what you want doesn't mean he's relaxed or thinking while he's doing it.

Anyone who thinks he knows everything he needs to know leaves no room to learn. Horses are not ATV's. They are a learning experience each and every day and it behooves us to take advantage of the opportunity. And it is to our detriment if we don't pay attention or take advantage of it.

HOWEVER, by following these steps, EVEN IF you don't believe or understand these concepts, just going through the motions with your horse will show you some of what's possible.

You have nothing to lose here and exceptional horsemanship to gain. Can you list five things about your horsemanship that you'd lose by trying this? Three? One?

Life is never something; it is merely the opportunity for something.

- Christian Hebbel

If you change the way you think about your horse, you'll change WHAT you think about your horse. Your horse will change what he thinks about you. Your horse will respect you and you will have respect for your horse. The relationship between the two of you will become what you didn't even know you always wanted.

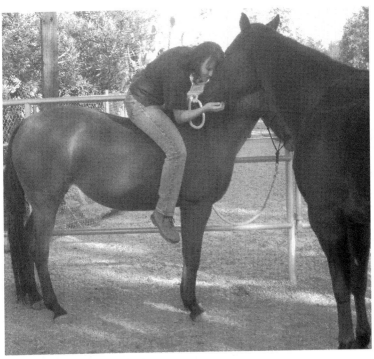

Courtney on Peka with Black Diamond. Yes, loose horses nuzzling you while the one you're on stays precisely positioned, not moving with a long, loopy line is fun.

Curbside Service

Would you want to miss out on discovering just how exceptional the relationship between your horse and you can be?

What Do You Think?

*Experience is not what happens
to a man; it is what a man does
with what happens to him.*

- Aldous Huxley

*Whenever you find yourself on
the side of the majority,
it is time to pause and reflect.*

- Mark Twain

3

Whys and Safety

Frankly, Curbside Service is a lot of fun and extremely convenient at horse gatherings of all kinds - shows, events, trail rides, etc. But there are myriad reasons for teaching this skill. Moving while mounting or dismounting is a safety issue. This skill also incorporates respect, direction and leadership, and is a points factor. From this one exercise, you and your horse also glean the knowledge, forethought and calmness to move his feet forward, backward, left and right, up and down. You will learn how to ask the horse to exhibit his skills correctly and precisely. You won't be pushing or placing your horse next to a fence or block. You will ask that he place himself. This is not difficult for the horse. It just seems to be difficult for people to understand that the horse finds this task quite easy. Once you see how easy it is for the horse to comprehend and execute this task, the building block for all the other tasks you will ever ask of your horse is in place. This concept and task/skill is a keystone!

This exercise starts you off in fantastic form and is one of the constants of learning the concepts needed to make phenomenal progress in your horsemanship. It is also a safety and convenience bonanza. Curbside Service and the concepts behind it have the ability to change the future of your life with horses.

Your horse's mental skills will amaze you. You will see how intelligent horses are while doing this exercise. Many horses are just playing 'possum with their people. It's part of their humor; enjoy it. It's also part of their coping skills, which you might want to be aware of, too. Enjoying your horse's humor makes your horse appreciate you more. He is a part of your time spent together, not just a toy or a pretty ATV. The training sessions are lighter and learning is facilitated...on both parts. Your horse will think you're smart and respect you more and vice versa.

Many times when I go sit on the fence where all my horses are loose, one or two of them will come over and present their back perfectly, offering for me to get on. It's a sweet feeling.

From a safety point of view, who would defend a horse walking or trotting off while it's being mounted? Yet most people either allow their horse to walk or trot off or they have someone hold the horse trying to keep it still. Can anyone hold 1100 pounds on four legs still by holding onto a clip under the chin? Not really. Hoof movement while people are holding their horses by or near the clip is rampant regardless of the task requested and is a clear disobedience, lack of training or both.

The underlying misconception is that the important stuff happens after you get on. But that's really jumping the gun. You do actually have to get on. With one foot up in the stirrup, your knee near your teeth, a hand on the rein and the mane, the other on the front of the saddle (if you mount properly) is it okay if he trots off? You bounce on one foot about 3 times for momentum and swing your leg over the horse. Your body is pitched forward in your most vulnerable position of the entire ride. Is it really okay if your horse just moves off while you're doing this?

> *Before you'll change,*
> *something important must be*
> *at risk.*

> - Richard Bach

From a different perspective, suppose you ask your horse to trot? Is it okay then if he canters? Or doesn't? In either case, the horse isn't doing what you ask. Why is there a difference when mounting? Curbside Service will improve your awareness and teach both you and the horse the value of Sit. Stay. Safety.

Precision is also a part of the safety issue. If your horse isn't in the right spot and you attempt to mount anyway, a greater possibility exists for a mishap. Again, if you don't correct it, it isn't a disobedience. Some people push their horse next to a mounting object and then the horse moves while the person is walking to the mounting side. The person doesn't want to get off the mounting block or fence, go around the horse, push the horse back into place and hope it stays. So he tries to get on with the horse too far away and puts himself in danger. Or, many times people step off the mounting block and move it to where the horse now is. Get back up on it and the horse moves again. Get down, move the block, ad nauseum. Meanwhile, the horse is cracking up with laughter. Likely, the horse will step even further away the second you start to throw a leg over, since he's never been trained and expected to stand still each time he's being mounted.

During your learning experience with Curb-side Service, you'll come to realize just how capable and precise your horse is. Safety in these instances should not be an issue. There is simply no need to put yourself in an unsafe position and there is no sense in giving your horse bonus points for bamboozling you.

Curbside Service also reduces or eliminates (depending on how high your mounting spot is) the torque on the horse's spine while being mounted. Consider how it feels to have 150 pounds or more pull the middle of your spine over to the side. Yes, it's nice to have the flexibility, strength, smoothness and balance to mount from the ground and sometimes there isn't anything to get up on or a place to put the horse down low. But reconsider if ego aspects are involved with "I can mount from the ground". In the hunter/jumper, dressage discipline, the horses are quite tall and it's common and easier for the rider to get a 'leg up'. But, this also requires a second person (who is frequently trying to hold onto a rein to keep the horse still also). Sadly, we've all seen the horse still walking off while the helper has a hold on the rein and the rider is still being given the leg up but not on yet. Dragging yourself up the side of the horse has a negative effect on the horse's spine regardless of your mounting skill and is worth some consideration.

Every horse I get in for training gets started with 'Curbside Service' training on the first day. Every horse. Even a one or two year old that isn't ready for riding. This is because the mindset/learning and skills needed for this task set you up for success from the get go. Any new students and their horses also learn this right away as it facilitates all future training and enjoyment.

**One task I generally spend some time on before teaching Curbside Service is leading. That's covered in another book in the

Horses have four different pages where they prioritize the tasks, behaviors and ideas you'd like them to perform and adhere to.

Page 4 is the "Not on your best day b..."(rhymes with witch)

Page 3 is "If you can make me".

Page 2 is "I will, but I won't like it".

Page 1: "Sure, you betcha".

Obviously, you would like as many tasks and behaviors as possible on the Sure, you betcha page, true or true? But what have you done to convince the horse that it would be beneficial for him to move a bunch of these tasks, etc. from one of the other three pages where they currently reside to the Sure, you betcha page? And does your horse even know that you don't care for that type of behavior?

Ideally, every time you work or play with your horse, you move a task, movement or attitude in some regard from page 2, 3 or 4 up a page or all the way to the "Sure, you betcha" page. It's important to know, though, that you are not privy to what is on what pages in the horse's book until it comes up while you're doing something with your horse. When you encounter resistance to a request, consider whether your horse understands the request or not. Have you ever worked on something like this before? If not, take the time to teach it now or put it on your list for another day.

If you have done it before, analyze on what page it seems your horse has listed this task, and then see what you can come up with to convince him to move it up a page or two.

series. Then the horse and I have set up a relationship and he understands giving to pressure and paying attention to what I'm asking. If the horse has decent ground manners and keeps a quiet, thinking mind, 5-10 minutes is all it takes to teach Curbside Service. If you haven't mastered the basic movements of forward, backward, left and right, or your horse isn't quite so good with instructions and thinking, it will take longer. But it's amazing how once the horse (and you) understands what the goal is, the horse easily puts it on the Sure, you betcha Page (see side bar).

Horses are a riot once you take notice. Unfortunately, many people generally miss their particular brand of humor. When people are the brunt of the horse's humor, folks are even less likely to see it or appreciate it. Until you accept it and start having fun with it, they will continue to get the better of you.

Once you do begin seeing the humor, you will enjoy your time with your horse more. Your perspective and the horse's frequently just aren't the same. Many horses operate with the majority of the tasks you ask them for assigned to pages 2 and 3. So we use all these mechanical devices (bits, spurs, whips, etc.) to make them do what we want them to do. This is a dreadful lack of communication, respect and trust! To change this we must change the way we think. Ignorance really is no excuse. This is also a dreadful lack of proper training and that dastardly excuse "We've always done it this way".

Experience means nothing.
You can bungle something for
thirty-five years.

-Kurt Tucholsky

From the horse's point of view, your use of bits, spurs, whips, tie-down and such, along with a lack of training or bad training is, in his mind, abuse. And can you blame him?

If you keep doing the same things TO your horse and treating him the same way, is he just going to wake up one morning and think, "Ya know, I've been awfully snarly with my person for the last 5 years. I think I'll just turn over a new leaf and be pleasant"? Nope, unlikely. Ear pinning, tail swishing and lifting a hoof are just a small part of the evidence of this need for change.

Let's change the way you think so your horse puts more things on the Sure, you Betcha page. Once your thinking changes, you will do things in a manner that accomplishes greater results, both in skills with your horse, your horse's behavior and the way your horse thinks about you. The interesting thing is that with this endeavor to teach your horse Curbside Service, it will change that way you think even if you didn't think so before.

A great way to change the way you think? Bareback.

This exercise is much more easily accomplished bareback. You can use a saddle, but it is less effective due to the timing, ease and flexibility of sliding on and off. The drag from the saddle and all those parts of the saddle get in the way for this particular exercise.

Equipment

As with most sporting activities, many different items are available and will get some results. Personally, I'm not real keen on 'some' results. Of course, you're going to get results regardless, good and bad. I want 'exceptional' results.

You can strap a couple of 2x4's to your feet and go down a snowy hill; but it's easier with skis!

Therefore, I recommend the basic natural horsemanship starter kit. A 12' yacht line lead, (preferably 5/8") although ½" is the more available size, a ¼" yacht line rope halter, a 4' stick with the 6' string attached. Personally, I don't like the stiff or really thin rope halters and I don't like the really soft ones either. I'm like Goldilocks; I want it just right. At the back of the book is a listing of my favorite places to obtain the equipment.

41

Curbside Service

If you are using a saddle because you've never or rarely ridden bareback, this is a good time to experiment with it as long as your horse isn't spooky to where it gives you concern. Interestingly, this is also a good way to de-spook horses. You will need some ability to climb on fences or whatever your chosen spot is and feel secure with jumping on and off the horse. Being on the fence and working on Curbside Service can be a very safe environment for the horse to learn de-spook skills. Make sure that your balance skills are adequate, though, to work on that with him. Do not rush any aspect of this and give yourself a thorough assessment. Don't be unsafe; develop safe skills. If you're a beginner, you may not want to do this without supervision or someone to help.

It's about taking the next step.

4

Show, Ask, Allow

Studies have been done; books have been written showing that, on average it takes a human 26 repetitions to learn something. Of course, some things are learned faster than others, usually depending on the level of interest or the consequences involved. So why do we insist that our horses learn what we want, in a language they don't speak, in one pull of the reins or kick of the boot?

I have seen people get on a horse that has never been ridden and kick him in the ribs to go. If someone kicked you in the ribs, would your first thought be, "Oh, sure, I'll just trot nicely around the arena for you"? My bet is no.

When teaching the horse something new, SHOW him in a clear, exaggerated format exactly what you want in small steps. Don't get ahead of yourself and expect him to come along with you when you haven't started at the bottom of the education ladder. The first step in the right direction or the movement is the first rung on the ladder. Relax and let him be still and process the situation when he gets the correct step or movement.

This way you won't instill panic and anxiety in the horse. If he gets worried, he may throw in every movement under the sun including the kitchen sink, hoping one of them is the answer. Maybe one of them is correct and he can do it fast enough before you swat him. So many people accept the whole array of kitchen paraphernalia thrown at them because one of them IS the answer. However, all the other things that aren't the answer are inappropriate, and the horse will not learn what the right answer is if all the extraneous, wrong answers are not eliminated.

As an example, many people ask their horse to back up, but the horse actually steps sideways. If the person never corrects the sideways movement, then when he asks for a back up again, a sideways movement is acceptable and even correct since that was the signal and the response that was accepted. If the horse does know how to back up straight and doesn't, and then isn't asked to correct his transgression, how many points do you think he gets?

Desire to have things done quickly prevents their being done thoroughly.

- Confucius

Slowly, move on to asking for the next single movement of one hoof and then relax again. This type of teaching will simplify and shorten any task you are attempting to teach even though many people believe that it's too slow. Hurrying things confuses the horse, and you'll end up spending a lot more time trying to fix it or giving up. Hurrying on the part of the person also frequently leads to incorrect positioning or too high a phase and then neither the horse or the person knows why this isn't going according to plan. Approach it properly in the first place.

Now, ask for a move forward one or two steps at a time. Relax and then ask for a move backward to the starting spot again. This lets the horse know it's the correct movement. Ask for the next movement, then go back and repeat. As you continue on to the completion of the task, remember you are going to ASK him to repeat it 4 times AFTER you're pretty sure the horse understands it. If, during the course of your 4 repetitions, he doesn't do it properly and needs your help, your counting starts over. This isn't an issue, just part of the training.

When you ask him for the movement, ALLOW him the time to process the request, think about the logistics of performing it and then begin the movement.

People haul their horses around with nasty bits in their mouth because they don't want to give the horse the time to perform the task. The speed with which you get a response from your horse is relevant to whether or not the horse understands what you are asking and how to perform it.

In people terms, I could grab your hand and stick it in a puddle of ketchup on your plate. Or I could ask you to put your hand in the ketchup. The difference is in whether I'm making you do something by force, or asking you to do something and then allowing you to do it, thereby soliciting your cooperation.

While having lunch with a friend/student and explaining this concept, the opportunity to explain it using the ketchup came up. The significance of the ketchup is that at times, we are going to ask our horses to do tasks that they may not want to do and we still would like them to do it, true or true? If I used a French fry as an example, it wouldn't convey the difficulty of convincing someone to do something undesirable.

Remember that I didn't say unsafe. I said undesirable. And this is frequently undesirable only because the horse has not been taught the requested move or hasn't been shown that there is no danger involved or a need for him to have an attitude about it.

In order to understand the concept for allowing, consider this; I may be able to get my friend's hand in the ketchup faster if I shove it in there, but I doubt I'll get cooperation. The more likely result will be malicious compliance, especially in the future. I may even get a tussle out of the deal. This is not the relationship I want from my horse. Yet, if I ask my friend to put her hand in the ketchup, she will need some time to process the request, then pick up her hand and put it in there. DON'T get in such a rush for immediacy. Allow your horse time to think about the request and then accomplish the goal. Remember the ketchup!

Martingales, tie-downs and draw reins are prime examples of making a horse do something through force instead of teaching him what you would like him to do and then asking him to do it. Humans are in such a hurry to get their own way. It's so much easier to strap a horse's head to his cinch than teach him to carry his head in an appropriate position and then asking him to do it. But what is the horse's opinion of having his head tied down? And what would your opinion be if your head were tied down?

*Inspiration cannot be willed,
although it can be wooed.*

-Anthony Storr

5

Here We Go

Objective: You walk to the mounting block/fence/rock/tailgate, etc of your choice, get up on it and your horse is ready and waiting at your knees to mount when you turn around.

What you do not do: you do NOT walk to your mounting block/fence in such a manner that places your horse on the 'line' next to the fence from which he would only need to move forward.

You do NOT circle to the other side of your horse and push him over near the fence and then try to climb up between him and the fence. You do NOT get in front and push or pull him backward or forward so he's standing where you need him to be to mount.

Depending on the training of the horse when I get him in, it generally takes me between 5 and 15 minutes to teach a horse how to Curbside Service. I have, on occasion, done it in about 45 seconds, though due to working with the horse for a little time beforehand. Obviously when both you and the horse are first learning, it's not going to be that quick. But, it's a pretty fast change-over.

After your horse understands this task, a mere click of your fingers or cluck of your tongue will be enough for him to make an adjustment should he be a little off the mark.

Have your stick with you the whole time while you're teaching. If you have to take the time to pick up your stick in order to make the correction, your timing will be late and the horse will not learn to be in the right place at the right time in an appropriate time frame.

To begin:

Find yourself a section of fence that you're comfortable sitting on. If you don't have one, you'll just have to make do with an uncomfortable one. It's best not to use a tailgate or mounting block for the initial training. The corners on a tailgate add an element of danger not worth messing with. A mounting block doesn't support you enough in the training as it allows the horse too much room to be in the wrong position. A trailer fender that you're comfortable standing on is okay if you don't have a fence panel area.

Once you've chosen your spot to perch for training, it's important that you understand that YOU are NOT going to place the horse in the correct spot. The goal is to go to your spot and expect the horse to place himself in the correct spot at your body.

Start about 20 feet perpendicular to your chosen fence spot. With the horse walking behind you on at least 6 feet of loose, droopy rope, head straight to the fence and climb up, turn around and sit. Stay.

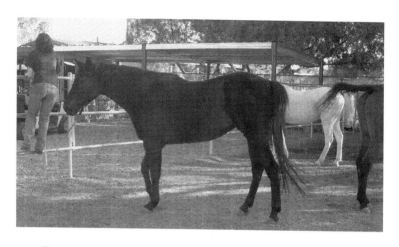

Courtney and Black Diamond on the approach.

Because most trained horses are more comfortable being mounted and handled on the left side, we're going to start there. But you and your horse should become proficient on both sides.

You're still sitting on the fence. Good! Your horse stands there quietly and you are able to flick the stick and string above, around and all over him without too much ado. If not, spend some time letting him know that it's okay. DO NOT keep a feel or contact on the lead. If you need to ask him to step closer, fine, but release the pressure on the line as soon as he moves in the correct direction and make sure he'll stand there with plenty of slack in the line.

Again, it is NOT your job to hold your horse still. It's your horse's job to stand still. This is an important concept for all your training, not just part of this task. I would like to emphasize this point. In people terms, if you knew how to do your job, would you like it and would it be productive if your boss stood over you and told you what to do next? No, if you understand your job, you want to do it without someone micro-managing you. Don't micro-manage your horse! The realization that horses don't need micro-managing is huge and oddly uncommon. Just wait 'til you see how good they really are.

Standing quietly on a long rope.

Back on the fence. With the lead in your left hand and your stick/string in the right, bring your left hand out to the left and in line with the fence. If necessary, shorten the distance on the lead to get the result you want, which is your horse's head at the fence to your left. Not over the fence, along side it. Make sure you release the pressure and allow slack back in the line when his head is where you want it. Ideally, the entire horse is completely straight along the fence. He may misunderstand at first, but it's really not that different from asking for any other movement. If you use your rope to get the front feet in the spot you want, but the head is over the fence, just poke/move the head back on the correct side of the fence until it stays there and then ask the hindquarters to get in line also. Again, this is no less important than any other movement.

Depending on where your horse is standing, you can drape the string over the right side of his back, or you can hold the string in your hand.

Now, tap the horse lightly on the right hip area until he starts to move his feet. If the back feet move toward you, immediately stop tapping. Sit. Stay. Rub your horse all over with the stick including the spot you were tapping. And repeat. You will continue this process until the horse is standing PERFECTLY next to the fence with his back RIGHT at your legs. If the horse is crooked or off the correct spot at the fence by even 5 inches, YOU ARE NOT DONE. It is imperative that you are precise about the SPOT where you want the horse to stand. If you aren't, you can't expect him to know or care exactly where to stand. Good enough for the government isn't applicable here. It's important that he knows exactly how precise you are going to be.

**Phyllis and Sassafras showing stick placement.
Sassy had just learned to Curbside with me minutes before in about 45 seconds and this is Phyllis'
first time doing it, too.**

If your horse moves in the opposite direction, DO NOT stop the tapping. If he's
moved too far away to reach the off-side

hip with the stick, gently, at first, swing the string over him at the right hip. If he continues to either not move in the correct direction or move in the wrong direction, keep up the signaling with your string. If you stop before he has tried to understand and/or move toward you, you will be telling him that it's okay to be doing what he's doing and not doing what you're asking him to do. You may need to 'up your phase' and get as strong as you need to cause him to think differently. However, don't get overly strong, as the horse needs time to process this new information and then figure out what you want and how to do it. Persist with an increase in the intensity of the energy and force only matching, plus a pinch more, the amount of the horse's resistance. Don't continue at the same intensity if the horse isn't trying. If this happens, he's showing you that what you're doing isn't working. You will need to change something, whether it's where your string/stick aim is or the intensity of the tap and your energy level. The horse needs to understand your aid/signal. But, his understanding is based on him, not what you think you need or want to do. People consistently over sig-nal their horses. They practically beat them over the head with a 2x4 and 99.9% of the time, this is not necessary.

As SOON as the horse moves one foot in the correct direction, stop what you're doing and pet him with the stick. Now take a rest. He does not need to be in the cor-rect position at the fence. All he needs to do is step one foot in the right direction. If you don't stop, he won't be able to figure out what maneuver you want. If he moves in the right direction and you keep tapping (at this training point), he will assume that that is not the answer since there was no re-ward (absence of tapping). Later on when he knows what to do and isn't in the correct spot, you can tap him over to the spot.

Don't get impatient. As I said before, horses get this in 5-15 minutes. If you lose your patience, the horse is then getting a different lesson. After a couple of days of consistency on your part, voila!!

Keep expecting the precise position. Don't settle for less. If the horse doesn't step over and align himself EXACTLY straight with the fence, ask again with a "Hey, excuse me sweetheart, don't know what distracted you, but you need to get your keester in the right spot". There is no good enough or close enough standard here. It needs to be SPOT ON!

There is more on precision and timing in Chapter 6 on corrections. Don't jump into this exercise before you read it as you will need to know this.

For both precision and time frame corrections, you're still sitting on the fence. Either circle the stick in the air above the horse's back or if that isn't enough encouragement, tap the far side or drape the string over him with a 'Say, how about movin' it' attitude. You may feel as if you're starting over, depending on the position of the horse. No, your horse may not be in the same spot you started, but this is just more of the training. If he didn't move over into the mounting position, just go back to the original training instructions and get him back to where he needs to be.

Your horse is standing at the fence. Now what?

Nothing. Absolutely nothing. You sit there on the fence. See why I said find a comfortable railing? And your horse stands there in the perfect position. And stands there. Sometimes it's a good idea to have a tidbit treat but!!! The horse can only move his neck and head to get the treat – not a hoof. If he moves a hoof, stop what you're doing, don't give him the treat and ask him to regain the proper position. Then give the treat. Each time the horse is standing quietly at the fence in the EXACT proper position, let him! Long line comfort just standing there is important. Then maybe he gets a treat. Soon, he'll look forward to being there.

You don't have any contact on the rope unless you need it for a quick signal or correction to move in a certain way. If he has drifted or repositioned incorrectly, get him back in position. Then make your rope loopy again. Drape it over the fence or just sit there with it in your hand, long and loopy. Take one of your feet and rub it on the horse's side, up, on and over his back and all over his butt. If he moves one foot (or more), stop what you're doing and ask him to regain his correct position. This may mean just the one hoof or you may end up getting the whole maneuver started again. No matter. This is part of the training for both of you.

Leg work while perfectly positioned next to the golf cart and on the horse's right/off side.

It's important to keep in mind at this point that you don't mind if the horse moves. RE-ALLY! It gives you opportunities to reinforce the specifics and precision of the task as you would like it performed. So don't get frustrated if he moves. You're getting it out now so you won't have to do it tomorrow. You actually WANT him to move sometimes so you can fix it. Problems are a chance for transformation.

The secret is "I don't mind what happens."

\- Krishmaurti

Choose different time frames for his standing. It may be a few seconds, a minute or quite a few minutes. After he seems to understand the concept well, slide your leg over his back until your butt just touches down and then slip right back up to the fence.

The idea is to get on and off before the horse moves. If he moves away from the fence, jump off and calmly walk back to the fence and start over. IT'S NO BIG DEAL! This is part of the process. It's just another opportunity to get your horse and you partnered up for exceptional horsemanship. Ask your horse to 'Curbside' with the lowest signal that gets the result. And slide your leg over, but not your butt. See if he'll move. If not, get back on the fence and give him a treat. And as long as he's standing there, practice sliding on and off again. If he doesn't seem inclined to move, take the opportunity to sit on him for some minutes. The instant he thinks about moving, either get back on the fence and correct the movement, or if he's quicker than that and too far away from the fence, just jump off and climb back on the fence and have him 'Curbside' again.

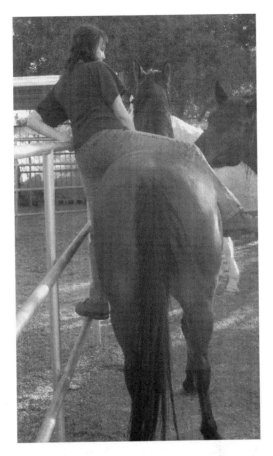

Courtney with Peka properly positioned for leg over work or mounting.

Regardless of whether your horse is bareback or saddled, spend some time jumping on and off. The next step is to jump off and walk off with your horse following.

Then head back to the fence, climb up and while climbing, cluck to your horse. He might just already be in position before you turn around. If not, ask him to step up to THE SPOT. This is what you're shooting for. When you climb up, your horse's back is right at your legs before you turn around. Repeat.

Now, it's time to slide on and sit there. And I do mean just sit there. You are not going anywhere, so don't. Do not pick up your lead line. Preferably it is 6 feet of loopy rope, with the other 6 feet just hanging there. It may be either over your horse's neck or just resting in your hand or even tossed in a loopy drape over the fence. Increase the time you spend sitting there, but if your horse is getting restless, get off before he moves his feet if at all possible. Again, if he's already moved, jump off and Curbside again.

Just sitting there.

At this time, while sitting on the fence, experiment with having him move off the fence at different angles. Back up, take a few steps forward, and any other direction and then have him come back to Curbside at your cluck. This exercise can get pretty extensive so allow time for all the opportunities for the two of you to be in different places and still get back to where you need to be. It also can get pretty fascinating. It's all part of the process. Don't blow through it unaware of the benefits. This is not to be hurried. It is to be repeated. Calmly and quietly. From multiple positions. Think of it like fishing, yo-yo or skipping rocks. Enjoy it.

The last paragraph is important and not to be left out of the training due to a particular safety issue. Sometimes, people get a little carried away with the horse snapping over rapidly. Then, the horse takes it upon himself to get even handier at this task and may decide that if you want him over there close and fast, he's going to show you just how close and fast he can be. You stand the risk of being smashed between the fence and the horse if you don't take the time to make it clear to your horse that he needs to move his feet when and where you ask and still be respectful. He doesn't need to come up with what he may consider a better answer for you. He needs to be soft and safe and if you don't like the position, he needs to alter it so it fits. This is where asking him to move on and off the fence comes in the training.

During this time of repetition and precision, change from using your stick to using your rope for the maneuver. Make sure you keep slack in the rope from your left hand to the horse's head and then use the remaining rope (it's so important to have a 12 foot line with some life in the feel) to sling it above and over to the right side of the horse's hip to get him to sidle over. If things get confused, whether you're having trouble with your operation of the line or if the horse doesn't seem to understand, you can go back to the stick to reinforce the training. After the stick and the rope are working well, move on to extending your right arm in front of you and clicking your fingers for the horse to move over to the correct Curbside position.

Phyllis with her rope.

Phyllis with her click while Sassafras starts over to her.

When practicing sliding on your horse during this time, don't always get on the moment he arrives at the fence. Vary the timing. Otherwise he may expect you to always get on immediately, and that just isn't his business. When you get on or if you get on is not his concern. Being in the proper position in case you WANT to get on is his concern.

Next on the agenda is to make movements while you're on your horse while he stands COMPLETELY still. Move your legs and arms and seat and head. Twist, turn, bump, poke (gentle pokes, of course, not 'go' pokes). All these movements don't mean go. They may mean go if that is your intent, but the horse must have the opportunity to learn the movements with and without intent so that he is able to discern the difference. If the horse moves one or more feet at any time, you must stop what you're doing and ask/insist that he move it right back and regain the original position at the fence. Do not continue out of position.

Once you and your horse have a great (and by this I mean not a hoof moves) result, it's time to pick up and drop the lead. Just because you pick up the lead or reins when you have mounted does not mean go. It may, but it should not be assumed. If you want your horse to step off when his rein moves and never ask him to discern differences, you should be sure you have this intent. By exposing him to the possibility that you might just need to move the rein, your horse will wait for you if he doesn't perceive the intent to move. He shouldn't be jumping the gun and deciding to go...anywhere!

For another example of how this "don't move" training comes in handy, picture a beautiful scenic area. You want to take pictures while mounted. You might want to rummage in your gear or change position to take the picture. You don't want Trigger jumping all over the place making your pictures blurry. While you're at it, you may want a drink or snack from your saddlebag. You may have found a distinctive branch of manzanita you want to tie onto your saddle. Or maybe you found a set of antlers. What if there's a bee buzzing around and you need to take a swipe at it? Dancing and spooking from your horse are not appreciated at these times. But if you never taught your horse to stand still, he's not going to. So it needs to be attended to before you're in that position. Do your homework at home.

When you have deliberate dawdling down to an art with the line or reins long and loose or picked up and dropped and your horse hasn't moved...it's time to ask him to move off and that's it!

*If you learn something new,
you are then required to
make mistakes in order to fully
understand what you have
learned.*

6

Corrections

Points

Horses beat dry British humor hands down. They are playing games and getting or giving points almost any time they're interacting with anyone - horse, human, dog, whatever. If you ask your horse to do something and he's busy reading the last chapter of *Black Beauty* and he doesn't put the book down, after carefully marking his page, of course, and give you some attention, he gets points. If you allow him to continue, he gets more points. If you can cause him to think that it would be better for him if he comfortably went along with you, you get points, etc.

You cannot rescind points; it's a done deal. You just need to make more points up on your side with what skills you have or create new skills to garner the points. You may as well acknowledge the points your horse wins when appropriate because he will assume and award the points regardless. If you don't know your horse is getting points, he gets double points. It doesn't matter to the horse what the reason is. He can gain the points due to your lack of knowledge, skills or awareness. Award yourself points, too, when appropriate, as your horse will award them to you also.

If you won't award points to your horse when he outmaneuvers you because you think that particular part of the game isn't point-worthy, you are mistaken. He still gets the points for outmaneuvering you, but that doesn't mean the game is over. The game is over when you leave the horse at the end of your time with him. So continue paying attention and gaining your own points until then. Smile when you realize that your horse got the points and maybe even say aloud, "Say, that was a good move. I'll give you 50 for that," and then a smile for yourself when you figure out how to balance that move with your own 50-75 point move.

Keep in mind that your horse frequently accrues many of these points before you even get on. This is especially true if he turns his butt toward you when you enter the stall. Maybe he puts his head up too high for you to comfortably reach while putting on the halter or perhaps he puts it too low also avoiding you. If he doesn't stand still or walks over you or ahead of you, he's thinking that this is going to be a good point-gathering time for him after you get on because you don't have the savvy to know he's getting all these points. And if you let it go, he's going to be sure you don't have the skills or commitment to fix it. Is that really how you want to start your ride? Behind?

Position concepts and corrections

Whose five inches is it anyway? This is a big points gathering situation! If your horse does not stand in the spot indicated, he gets points. The fact that it's possible to swing your leg over his back while your horse is crooked and some feet or inches away from where you asked him to stand isn't the point. The point is that he isn't where you asked him to stand or where he knows you expect him to stand. Precision and compliance are important in this instance because they represent respect, points and safety all in one fell swoop. This isn't an area to ignore.

If he knows where to be and isn't there, he gets all the points. Even one leg sticking out sideways counts as points for him. Obviously he could have placed the hoof in line just as easily, right? Yet, he chose to set it down otherwise.

If you would like a clearer indication of how precise your horse can be, try this exercise. Get two plastic flat discs such as a gallon tub container lid or a frisbee. Lay them on the ground about six feet apart. While you have your horse on a line and you have your stick and string with you, stand on one disc and see if you can cause your horse to place a hoof, any hoof, on the other disc.

Corrections

You may not move from your disc. You see how good your horse is at maneuvering his feet. After you have successfully gotten one of his feet on the disc, try getting the other three on there in turn. Then, to challenge yourself, pick a hoof and that is the only one that he can place on the disc. If you think standing on the disc is too hard at first, try to get the horse to place his foot on the disc while you have the freedom to move around.

Hint: Remember, you have forward, backward, left, right and around.

It may amaze you to find that your horse can avoid the disc, sometimes by 1/16th of an inch while it's behind his hoof, maybe under his belly, and he can't even really see it. They can be VERY precise.

There is no reason to be unclear here. Both you and your horse need your mental and physical precision. Five inches is the difference between solid ground and the 1000-foot drop precipice (less than that if you're at the Grand Canyon. More like 1 inch, eh?). If you don't practice precision, you're not going to get it when you need or want it. Your horse will be saying to himself, "Well, I never did exactly as you asked before; I'm not apt to do it now." You must set the precedent beforehand.

If you're inclined to let a few inches go here and there, ask yourself why and then ask yourself if that spot isn't important, couldn't the horse be yet another eight inches away from there? Don't be sloppy; it's just not worth it. Precision is imperative. On that cliff edge is not the place for the first steps in training.

Timing

Time frame is so important. Once the horse understands what is expected, there is no reason for him to be lollygagging. There is no need for a horse that's going to be moving over anyway (remember your precision) to gain extra points by lollygagging.

Of course, the horse needs to be completely sure of the task you're asking him to accomplish before you institute a change in the timing. Take the time required now! If the horse doesn't understand what you want him to do and you continue to ask him to try, that's one thing and as it should be. But to ask him to perform a task he doesn't understand faster is foolish.

*There is more to life than
increasing its speed.*

- Mohandas Gandhi

Once he does understand and you have repeated the steps enough times so you know it's clear, then is the time to say, "Hey, I'd appreciate it if you would step it up a bit, precious."

If any holes in the training show up, make sure you slow it down and go over it again so signals and desired results are clear. Then you can tap the ground or the part of him that you want to respond with the stick or string or signal at a little higher energy and phase to accomplish the request in a suitable time frame. This does not mean suitable to your horse. It doesn't take but a few seconds to move a few feet, so he needn't lollygag, smoke a cigarette and blow the smoke rings in your face before he complies. A three-count is usually enough time to allow him to process the request and begin to comply. After that, increase your signal, intensity or energy asking in a stronger way for him to accomplish the goal.

Always give yourself the once-over to determine if you may be out of position. Position analyzing can be very difficult for people when they are first learning and dealing with these concepts and this is where someone who knows these concepts is helpful as an observer. You want to be sure that you are in the right place, focused or tapping the correct area and not being unclear. It isn't fair to correct the horse when he can't understand what you're asking. But if he's not trying to understand you and you are being clear, that is a different story. The best indicator of whether or not you may be out of position is the horse. He won't do the movement correctly, but he thinks he is because he's read your position to mean that. Try moving slightly and see if that helps. Check the points value and who is accruing them. Are the points yours or his?

Another way to advance your position knowledge is to watch horses interact with each other. Watch what they do and how they do it. How do they interact with each other? How do they position themselves in both dominant and subservient positions? In addition, you can move around in the middle of a group of horses and watch what your position does and what happens when you lift an arm here or there or move into a different space.

Voice

When you're correcting a horse, it's important to keep a casual voice tone (both spoken and in your head) and choose your thoughts and word selection carefully. This really improves your horsemanship. Examples are included throughout the book of what to say under certain circumstances because results are affected by what you say and how you say it and the inner feeling you are associating with the request. Calling your horse sweetheart or darlin' is a much better feeling than some words you may think of calling your horse. It keeps you calm and soft and the horse responds better. What type of tone and word choice would you respond better to if your boss were correcting you?

Horses don't communicate with each other by voice for the most part. They call to a buddy who is leaving or returning or nicker to the person they like or when the feed comes. These are occasions where some distance is involved for the most part. Horses don't call to horses standing right next to them to say, "Move your keester!" In general, any voice commands you teach your horse relate to your horse learning to speak your language. Body position and energy are what horses really pick up on and humans are less inclined to be as astute in this area. It does take some training and frequently someone aware of these attributes to point them out to many horse owners. An interpreter, someone who has spent time observing horses, may be helpful. Or if you have the opportunity, watch horses when they're out loose together.

The reason I mention voice in the beginning of this section is because it's helpful to YOU. There is a internal feeling involved when you choose certain words and tones that helps you keep a balanced mental feel that promotes success instead of anger which can cause a mess with your horse.

It's a great signal to cluck your tongue once when you ask the horse to come over. Re-read the previous line again. How many times do you cluck? Once! None of that repetitive cluck, cluck, cluck or kiss, kiss, kiss. One single sound at a time. You may need to cluck again for the signal, but don't do it more than once at a time. Multiple clucks is nagging! If he doesn't respond with one cluck, you're teaching him he doesn't have to comply if you cluck even more. It's important to your training and the horse's that you don't over signal or allow your horse to think that you will. There is no reason that multiple clucks should convince or bribe your horse into thinking that he should comply. He can just as easily comply with one cluck. If you cluck more than once and don't get a response, he gets extra points. If he doesn't respond to the cluck, then it must be followed up with a backup signal to encourage him to follow through and then only need to cluck the next time you ask.

It may help to think that during each ride you have a small "bag of clucks". You only have so many in the bag each time you're with your horse. You don't want to waste them carelessly and all at once and not have one left when you need it.

If you have asked the horse to get in position and he has not complied, the next phase is to up the energy and execution of the signal. There is never any anger involved in a correction. If you're angry, it's not a correction; it's a punishment. A horse will give another horse several signals before the bite or kick, but once the other horse understands, all it takes is a look. Likewise, sometimes your signal might be pretty strong – but just until the result is effected. You always want to start with the smallest signal. Give your horse the chance to respond. Ask and allow, rather than start your signal and phase too high and hard, then when your horse loses his mind, you say, "Oops, too much."

If you're worried about the strength of the signal, as long as you're not "going after" the horse or angry, think of it like this. You are going to aim your string at a spot in the air or on the ground. You are not going to swat the horse; you are going to swat the spot. Now a part of your horse may currently reside in that particular spot. But, if your horse moves before the string gets there, mission accomplished. If he doesn't move, he chose to stay there when he had already been asked to move and didn't. If he hadn't stayed there, the string would not have connected with him. It is important to maintain a neutral tone and feel, no anger, while performing these movements. It's also important to practice your movements with the equipment so you can actually hit your target.

If you over-shoot occasionally or your aim is off, it won't be the end of the world. If you operate with high phases and energy, or you hit your horse due to poor marksmanship, your horse will not trust or respect you. And rightly so. Be mindful of the horse's response so you know if you signaled appropriately.

People frequently use what they think is the smallest signal, but for the horse it's huge or too much. Reducing your signaling is a goal to consistently strive for. Do less; expect the same or a better result. If you observe your horse, you should be able to discern whether your HORSE thinks the signal was too high, not you. Watch the eyes and ears and pay attention to the degree of anxiety or the reaction speed to your signal. Speed isn't a good thing if your horse does multiple movements, hoping one of them will be the right answer or maybe not even caring if one of them is the right move, just that you accept any movement. Your horse is the one who gets to decide whether a signal is enough and what is too much, not you. If he is excited or scared, don't automatically expect him to get used to your signal. Ask yourself if you might be using too much signal. Try reducing it and monitor the response. Conversely, if you aren't getting a response you will then need to increase the intent, energy and the signal.

At times, the signal or touch may be quite strong, as horse-to-horse instruction will sometimes be. But the human's job is to focus on making sure that each successive signal or touch from the human becomes lighter and lighter until it's no more than a wisp.

Note: These concepts for horses and people and the importance of precision are covered in more detail in the book *'til I Came to Realize*.

*It is vain to do with more what
can be done with less.*

-William of Occam

*The secret of success is
constancy to purpose.*

-Disraeli

7

Woo-Hoo

You've done it! Your horse follows you to whatever you step up on and maneuvers himself into position with the center of his back at your legs before you even turn around from climbing up on the fence. He stands there waiting for you to do whatever it is you want to do. Or he stands there while you do nothing. Congratulations!

Since most people are more comfortable mounting from the left side, even if you have an untrained horse, it's generally easier to start the training on the left. In any case, to avoid confusion, it's easier if you do NOT work both sides right away.

Stay with one side for a week or two so it's cemented and easy for both of you. When you do decide to teach the other side, allow plenty of time because the horse will think that you've lost your mind and don't know what you're asking. He'll repeatedly say to you with his movement, "This is how we do it," and you will have to repeatedly say, "That was before; now I'm asking you to do it this way." Sometimes teaching the other side can be tougher than the first side.

Gryffindor positioned perfectly while Courtney mounts from the 'other' side.

In your training, consistency is important. Maintain these same principles and vary your time frames checking to see if some reminder needs to be applied. This is also because you want to be able to change things up and have your horse respond appropriately. Should the horse move when you didn't ask for it, DO NOT let it slide unless you're in a life-threatening situation like a stampede. The correction of moving back to the original position is important. It only takes a second, but if you don't do it, your horse will know that you are not on your game today and will be ahead of you in the points system before you've even started. Then he will attempt more movements to gain points in other ways.

These concepts apply to all tasks and encounters with your horse. If you aren't paying attention, know full well that your horse is. You will come out on the short end. You may not even know you're on the short end, but your horse does. Even though you may not get hurt that time, down the road it will be important. If you do not maintain an attitude of precision and consistency, you won't get the desired response from your horse under adverse conditions. Everyone dodges a bullet occasionally, but we can reduce our chances of being shot.

The ramifications of low percentage results could be something such as falling off that Grand Canyon precipice or getting caught in a pack in the show ring. In the show ring, the horses may panic due to the quite real possibility of getting kicked while boxed in. Maybe you're out on trail and someone goes tearing by you on a galloping horse. Or a neighborhood dog gets loose and comes after you. Will your horse do what you want under any of these scenarios?

In a panic situation, it's likely that you may only get 50% of a movement at most, due to the state of your mind, the energy of the moment and your horse's state of mind. If your precision is so poor in your regular riding and training that a movement or your ability to keep your horse's attention is only at 10%, you're only going to get maybe at best half of that. Is 0-5% good enough to get you out of a crisis situation? Don't think so.

Don't settle for low expectations. Low expectations result in sub-par results. Expect more. It doesn't take any more time to be aware of what's happening with your horse. You're already there while you're with him, but BE with him. Pay attention! It's paying attention to the little things that make the big things go well. Paying attention becomes second nature. Then you can do all those other things and still be aware of what's going on underneath.

Go for excellence from yourself and your horse, and then enjoy this partnership with your horse.

*Excellence is not a singular act,
but a habit.*

- Aristotle

The horse is God's gift to man.

- Arabian Proverb

Afterword

I wrote this book while spending 3 months hooked up to two machines with a completely broken knee. Surgeon said I could probably start getting on a horse in 6–7 months. So, I got on after three months. I figured that if I could start walking, I could start riding.

However, since I'm in a brace and had no ligaments attached and no muscle strength, I would not have been able to mount or dismount if all my horses and the horses I work with (student's and trainees) didn't provide Curbside Service.

Curbside Service is also a must for therapy horses. The positioning for mounting and dismounting in addition to the safety and movement or non-movement of each and every hoof and the respect required to attain this that comes from Curbside Service training is invaluable.

☙❧

Resources

I prefer a 5/8" yacht /marine line for the 12 foot and 22 foot ropes as the weight, feel and width give better results than any other size. It is difficult or impossible to find, so I make them myself. Contact me at lauren@ exceptionalhorsemanship.com for info.

Horsefriendly.com

Excellent weight and feel and rope size for halters. Stick and string are good and the pricing is usually the best. Their 12' rope only comes in ½" which is a bit light and narrow. Color selection for ropes is broad. Service is excellent.

Parelli.com

Came up with the standards. Now uses a ½" rope instead of the original ¾". Halters tend to run a little small. Pricing is expensive.

Downunder Horsemanship/Clinton Anderson

Good selection of items. Ropes tend to be a bit fuzzy and are 2 feet longer. Some items are a bit pricey.

Google "natural horse tack" for more options, but always check the specifications of the materials and sizes.

❧